Envision & Wonder

Founder | CEO | Creative Director | Lovietta Simpkins
Editor in Chief | Leevette Simpkins
Literary & Creative Agent | Travis Walker
Author | VTA (Vince the Artist)

This work of poetry is based on a true story as told by author Vincent Burgess Jr.

Envision & Wonder
First Edition Month & Year: May 2019
Publisher: Envision & Wonder
ISBN: 978-0-9961561-5-8

Dedicated To My Big Brother,
"Terry Toliver."
2/3/84 - 3/6/19

IT'S PERSONAL

VTA

Table of Contents

RELATIONSHIP

RELATIVE

Table of Contents Continued

RELATIVE CONTINUED

REALITY

IT'S PERSONAL

RELATIONSHIP

REMARKABLE

Ok baby I feel you, don't wish you harm,
but I just wanna heal you.

You can be my nightmare and I will fear you, play your
favorite sport watch me cheer for you.

Make me your king cause every queen deserve one, I'm only
focused on where we going who cares where you came from.

God took his time creating you that I know and believe is true,
me losing you is frightening so I promise no more fighting it's
destine that we be together cause we like thunder and lighting.

Everyday I see you is a cause for celebration cause you mean
the world to me you my dedication.

I know I got the best woman smooth skin with a smile that
makes you so adorable, me not lifting you up everyday of my
life is impossible, not only did God make you for me, but he
made you remarkable.

IMPRISONMENT

Some say patience is the key you feel.

I sting your heart with my love so I die like a bee, but you want me to believe all the things you telling me I'm all for expensive actions cause baby talk is cheap, it seem like a dream an unwanted fantasy, us happy never sad how nice would that be.

Different emotions that ends with I don't care main reason cause the outcome wasn't fare.

It's ok that you didn't wanna give me that commitment, I need a way out cause I'm fed up with this feeling of imprisonment.

LET YOU KNOW

When I look at you all I see is truth, with your eyes you smile I like the clothes you wear and your hair style.

I know he did but I wouldn't lie to you, I put my arms around you so I could hug you, bring your lips closer so I could kiss you, I can't take my eyes off you because your beautiful, if you leave just for a second I text hurry back cause I miss you, when you pissed I get pissed too.

No matter how mad I get I'm going to stand by you regardless, the only way I can stop loving you is when I'm cold stiff and heartless, I cut through the tension like a blade with excellent sharpness, I'll be your light to guide you out the darkness.

I'm the seed in your garden of love and everyday I'm with you, you make it grow, you my lucky charm that I'll always keep and never let go, I could have kept these feelings to myself, but I think that it's best for me to let you know.

I DO

When I met you I wasn't scared, but I acted scary,
I told myself that all your burdens I wanna carry, I knew we
would go good together like the word straw and berry,
I'm not the type to move fast but no lie
I wanted to skip dating and go straight to getting married,
make that promise of death do us part until I or you they bury.

My love for you girl is so deep that I believe with you by my side
I could breath below the sea, I trust in you with my heart and soul
the same as my religious beliefs, I wanna get to know you a lot
better then you know me, I wanna watch you when you walk
watch your lips when you talk like a movie.

I don't want you to bring the good or the best out but the
greatness that's in me, when I don't see or hear from my queen I
die on the inside and they ask y but then they say o because they
know the reason being is because of you.

I'm thankful for what I have and I don't never want to realize
what I had that's the truth. I'm gonna treat you right I'm gone
miss you call you text you kiss you as if I wished I still could
when I lost you while I still have you.

Look into my eyes listen to my heart as it beat for us my words
my actions is the proof, I'm sure curiosity crosses your mind
wondering if this is to good to be true. We both may remember
but can't look back on the past we gotta look forward to the new,
I can't wait to see you in that dress and you see me in that suit
cause that's the day we say these three letters and two words I do.

FIRST LOVE

I heard you was sick so I'm writing you this letter I'm drawing
kiss lips on paper hoping it make you feel better.

When we laugh and hug it makes me feel good I understand
you cause others misunderstood.

It was a lesson I had to learn and that I'll never forget because
of that I got the girl I always wanted to be with.

I never wanted to break up never want things to change so
even when I mess up tell me to get up, so I can shape up, and
after that, that's when we make up. Balloons cake hugs and
handshakes got us the date that we both celebrate.

Only thing I want on top of us is the roof we have together and
the sky above, I am yours and you are my first love.

IN LOVE WITH THE NIGHT

Introduce myself to you like hi and how do you do, you look at
me strange cause you think I'm running game.

I'm telling you now I'll never switch up and that I stay in my
lane, I think for myself I use my own brain.

I'm trying to show you I care and not all guys the same, no
matter when we fight my feelings for you want change, I use to
have heart aces feeling major pain.

When I give gifts, it's not to hide what I'm doing, money and
bright future is all I'm pursuing.

You being lied too feelings played with happened too many
times, I understand cause your feelings got played with
just like mines, people never want you
during the struggle only in your prime.

You too precious to hurt and why would I knowing this is real,
your heart been broken and still until this day it never fully
healed, so I couldn't do that to you cause
I know how it feel.

We can go where ever you like, just pack your bags
so we can take flight, get a blanket and a basket
so we can lay under the stars
and fall in love with the night.

TRUST YOU

Your phone ringing you scared to answer cause I'm around,
I'm not stupid I pay attention so how you sound, I was buried
under your deceitfulness but now I'm rising out the ground.

You got a missed call and a text too, you look at it trying to
play it off but you better respond to your boo, you telling me
he just a friend and nothing more, you treat him with royalty
and treat me like I'm poor.

I talk to you with kindness, you know
all his favorites but don't know what mine is.

Late night calls that you answer in the other room and you not
even being sneaky, you tell me you couldn't answer
or reply to me cause you was sleepy.

That was you who said cheating is wrong which is true,
but I guess it's only wrong when it's being done to you.

Too many times you said I'm at work I'm out with my friends
but whole time you was with him, I try to treat you right and
be a good man that you need but you want the pimp.

I did a you on you and now you wanna blame who, it's cause of
what you did and the way you act that I can't trust you.

GENTLEMEN

I have to ask how you doing, when you say nothing I wish I can
do nothing with you, send the poke lip emoji since I can't
actually kiss you, I don't know why you
think I'm lying when I say I miss you.

Stutter with my words when I see it's you, open the car door
for you and I hold other doors too.

When you don't have it just know I do, don't need many
friends a click or a crew, I only want it to be just me and you.

I bend over backwards for you go above and beyond so you
want cry, I know I can't keep you happy everyday
but I know I can try.

I'm not trying to play with your mind or waste your time, I just
want to make you laugh and make you mine.

I cant be like other guys give just to get some in return cause
that wouldn't be genuine, I cant be rude
I have to be a gentleman.

I LIKE YOU

I wanna do things but not to upset you, I'ma get your attention
just by me staring at you, promise it want be harsh if I ever
decide to test you, first thing next day good morning beautiful
is what I text you, I thank god for us meeting
and me having you.

I make time for you and I hope you do the same for me, flowers
cards and favorite candy I bring, I want something real
not a one night thing.

I wanna say you mines and not she was just a fling, I wanna
turn that promise and into a wedding ring, I'm ready for the
hard work with all the pain and suffering, I wanna have your
heart racing and I'm the reason behind it. Other guys said what
they said it was all lies but my every word is true, I do what I
do because I like you.

ON MY MIND

I wanna talk to you, but I don't know what to talk about, I just
wanna see you smile make you laugh when I take you out,
I'm interested in your biography cause I get to know you, what
makes you cry, what gives you butterflies,
let's talk all night
and be surprised how time fly.

Let's take a trip face the window and see the clouds in the sky,
what's yo favorite movie,
seeing how you react to the screen does something to me,
I wanna know your secrets, I want that exclusive us only club,
let's change that I like to I love.

What are your goals and your dream,
voice in your head telling you baby you got this
you can do it
is me,
go out with your friends have girl time
your no hostage,
you free.

No matter how many gifts I buy
and the amount of money I have it isn't the same as me
spending time, these are all the things I want you to know, the
things that are on my mind.

POEM DESCRIPTIONS

REMARKABLE
This poem is about a man expressing how special,
how different and how grateful he is to have such a
remarkable woman.

IMPRISONMENT
This poem is about being trapped in your own thoughts of how
someone else did you wrong and trying to find reasons why.

LET YOU KNOW
This poem Is about a guy who wants to tell his girl how he feels
or how he has been feeling about her.

I DO
This poem is about a man telling his woman all the reasons
why he can not wait to say I do to her.

FIRST LOVE
This poem is just basically talking about the first time he felt
love and the things that he is doing, is because of love.

IN LOVE WITH THE NIGHT
This poem is about making sure your girl know you want hurt
her like the people or person before you cause you felt the
same pain.

TRUST YOU
This poem is about having issues with trusting.

GENTLEMEN
This poem is simply about being a good man.

I Like You
This poem's about a guy sharing with his crush what he wants to do now and in the future.

On My Mind
This poem is about a man who is trying to relieve his mind from thoughts he has been having about his girlfriend.

IT'S PERSONAL

RELATIVE

INVISIBLE

Hurt is a feeling that I often feel my inside is like an orange that you can't see unless you peel. They talk about me when I'm up but even more when I fall, I laugh as though I'm really happy when I'm not at all.

Funny how people say you have no reason to be sad it's like they force me to smile when I choose to be mad, you can't change the world to good when certain things made it bad.

Yes it would be nice for things I want to come easy but it'll be hard to keep, people please understand I'm not asking and no I don't need your sympathy.

Don't say you get it you feel my pain when you don't cause you're not me, yeah others been through too maybe worse but we all got different out looks we original not a copy.

If I had a wish it'll be to become the hulk so when I get angry I can let out my frustrations and be invincible, sometimes people don't hear me out so it seem that I'm not seen and that's cause I'm invisible.

JUST AIN'T RIGHT

The man you say you had use to treat you like your dad, got
you feeling lonely and unwanted always made you mad, daddy
and him both told you that you they wish they never had, the
wrong that was done it was all on you it was never they bad.

Now you older things changed nothing feels the same, even
when a person tells you I love you makes you feel strange.

Why you do it I know your past men hurt you but every man
deserves a chance so don't judge him on a unthinkable sin,
he'll understand that before him
you lost but now with him you can win.

He's the man that say your last battle you fought a good fight,
but don't deny the Opportunity of a person to really love and
care for you cause that just ain't right.

GUILTY

To the judges family friends my girl and all the use to be, I stand before you today because I have some wise words to say, it's about me and how I see things so nothing that I write nothing that I do is always about you.

I take full responsibility for my actions, it wasn't the real me I was only acting. If people choose to rush things to happen now and be wild continue to miss behave, please know that disappointments will come quicker including an early grave.

I understand people will forget what I've done for them and tell me I did nothing, Its all lies they just fronting.

I do admit I made a mess and I can't clean things up so I will leave it filthy, I said some things and done some things I shouldn't have and I apologize but if you're going to judge me on that then I'm guilty.

LAID IT ALL OUT

I might not be confident or talk with confidence maybe
because I get no compliments, I receive nothing but bad
comments. I count myself out before I even start, everything
moves slow all except my heart.

I wish I could take another approach like just stare or wink,
but before I say anything I convince myself that I already know
what you are going to say or think.

I'm insecure so my insecurity is taking over me, sometimes
who you are isn't who you wanna be, yes I'm the definition of
loyalty, she got no problem being loyal to him so why she
couldn't stay loyal to me.

The way that I am is because of my track record, I wanna be
salt but I'm stuck as the black pepper, I doubt myself to much
which isn't good and I know better, at night I pray the prayer
the Lord is my Sheppard, I have difficulties helping myself but
with others I do so I'm still a helper.

I'm the only one searching for the new me so I don't need a
scout, I wanted you to sit close to talk face to face so I wouldn't
need to shout, I told you every reason why I am the way I am
it's nothing more to add because I laid it all out.

A LIL CONFUSED

We meet say hi deep conversation, don't wanna say bye seeing
and hearing from each other give us that high, the past seem
irrelevant but a curious mind make us question why.

You seem so unreal so I wanna know what happened before me
how did it end was it a tragedy and if it was no need to worry
now cause you got me.

You start by saying he was cheating and lying always had you
crying never wanted to spend time he speak soft and low you
said huh and he said never mind, you stayed even though he
wasn't trying, girl you was blind.

Ask that guy to explain why he caused you harm and pain, you
was willing to work things out with someone who
didn't wanna work things out.

You cried over a guy who never shed a tear for you, but you
laugh at a guy who biggest fear is losing you, so you telling me
you believe in false more then truth.

It's OK to give a second chance when he don't deserve it,
but it's not to give the same chance to the guy who hurting,
he gave his all
willing to give his life
but he's worthless,
and the guy who gave nothing but short convo and sex
is worth it.

Just cause you got his baby now you wanna be his wife what
about the one who was gonna do the same
but you blew out the candle light,
the beginning you gave good intentions
but I'm starting to see some of the things you doing
you forgot to mention just when you say I didn't know,
now you know that I was paying attention, thought it was only
my time but it was my heart that I was really risking.

Gotta admit you made a good move but in the end I won and
you lose that's why you in a bad mood miserable in the
bedroom, crying in the bathroom.

You had real and true love when you had me
but you wanted him and now you feel used.

You made all those accusation about me doing things when it
was you and that got me a Lil confused.

DON'T CRY

Dedicated To My Big Brother
"Terry Toliver"
2/3/84 - 3/6/19

I apologize to my family and friends cause I didn't mean to do it,
it wasn't like I said I'm ready so screw it.

Your going to miss me and I'm going to miss you, forget the bad
times let's talk about the times that we had a ball.

Remember my jokes and remember my smile, I had so much fun
and probably got a little to wild, hope you see me
when you look at my child.

To all my home boys, yea I remember them days, and just cause
I'm gone doesn't mean you forget them days, I'm not going to say
a name but shorty you know you had some crazy ways.

To my sister and my brother you got on my nerves but I love you
to death, and even though death came to get me
doesn't mean it isn't any love left.

I'm here for you in spirit so I'm all around, I'm not just in a
cemetery laying under ground. I hope you continue to live life to
the fullest like I lived mine, we all got that hour glass of life and
God told me I'm out of time.

Don't be mad at me or God and ask him why,
cause at some point of time we all gotta die, I'm finally happy
now so please don't cry.

HONEST

Um ok where should I start I'm gone take a real good swing
and knock it out the park, during the day my mind standing
still but it's full speed after dark.

I get creative with it call me Tony Stark, all I need is you and a
little spark. We got beef let's settle it no guns no knife, you was
something I loved and I was something you liked.

For some reason I was always wrong but you was always right,
wanted you for life not like him who wanted you for one night.

The kisses from your lips to mines blows my mind, you was
something special I'm talking one of a kind, you're cute and
you're also fine.

See what you say about me, I'm gone say about you, what you
think about me, I'm gone think about you, how you feel about
me, I'm gone feel the same for you, and if you miss me, then
baby I miss you too.

Some days be good and some days be bad, they say it's better
to be mad then to always wonder, a lot of guys want you so I
guess I'll take a number.

I know I'm not the worst and I'm not perfect either, I put so
much pressure on myself I think it's time for a breather.
I know I'm not the funniest, things I say may seem unreal, but
this is me just being honest.

ALONE

They say in life you should want the finer things I'm in
constant thought defining things, it's all scribbled up and kind
of confusing, my asking turned to begging but still refusing,
every time I think I'm winning,
turns out I'm really losing,
my words come from my heart,
so that's what I'm using.

When you die it's only you in that casket,
if you got a question don't be scared to ask it.

I say what I mean, and I mean what I say,
but what ever I say you say I'm mean.

I never been weak I always been strong,
I cry on the inside cause I don't want it to be shown,
I was born and I'm living this way
but I don't want to die alone.

MY CONFESSION

Do you want to know, no really do you. If you dislike me f u screw you, let me do me like how you wanted to do you. On my death bed of life I still fight even if they don't want me to pull through, people see me they judge but they don't have a clue.

I'm trying to stay together but I'm gone need more then glue,
I'm gone need more then you,
I'm gone need more then who,
I'm talking to myself in the mirror,
the problem is me it couldn't be any clearer.

Day in day out my dreams I fight with, people turned they back on me thoughts of why just want quit, I said ok I'm done that's it. Days later those same thoughts and question starts again, I finally realized that all I have is me in the end.

I'm done trying to be some I'm not putting on impressions, I dragged myself out some how when I was dealing with depression, am I wrong for being mad at myself at the world and having aggression,
after my struggles the hurt and fingers being pointed at me I made some progression,
I know a lot of people won't agree with what I'm saying
or hate that I'm saying it
but these are my confessions.

QUIET PLACE

I need a peace of mind, if I can swap brains I'll give you mine, I
would settle for half just to save time.

People, work and life itself gives me a headache, I love all no
matter what, make no mistake, I'm tired of fighting for food
just so others can steal it off my plate.

It's hard not to say nothing so I get angry and shake,
my blood and muscles don't know how to act,
they think it's an earthquake.

To many problems I can't handle I have to share this, they
think I'm crazy saying I need a therapist,
I'm stuck reliving memories this got to be a glitch.

My eyes burn
from tears
they feel like they were sprayed with mace,
I lost me
I have no flowers
no water,
I'm just a empty vase,
giving me a room with nothing
is nothing but space,
what I need is mental,
so mentally where is my quiet place.

I DON'T GET

On earth I think I'm supposed to be a motivational speaker.

I think that's my mission,
we living in a generation that's very confused and twisted,
the knowledge was passed down to us
and some how we missed it.

I see a lot read a lot
and hear a lot of things that people ignore,
everybody holding grudges this
and that person hate
only with each other we at war.

To many females say I wish I had a man
to hold,
to kiss, and cuddle with
and rub my feet,
but y'all keep falling for the same type of guy
that aggressive type that can't stay in the house to watch tv.

Over half the world wanna turn up girls and guys doing things
they never done,
they become a follower
following the followers
doing what everybody else do

just to blend in exactly where they don't fit in.
I know people are gonna talk have some bad to say about this
or me, but I don't care this my poem this how I express my
thoughts in my poetry.

If you're tired of the same thing pick up the new and the old
just quit,
but no you rather keep the tears,
the stress and all the problems
that you don't have to put with,
only to please your friends or your family
and that right there I don't get.

COLLEGE DEGREE

Running down the hall when I should be walking,
open the door to the class and nobody talking.

I get to my seat to have a seat and prepare for greatness, it's
going to take hard work and a lot years but I'm patient.

I'm real about my future while some just fake it,
some people don't but I want to make it,
cross that stage and yell yes I made it,
if you don't believe or have nothin' good to say
you can save it,
I will succeed and yes I claim it.

I know it's not easy writing paper after paper,
but at the end of it all you gon' be making that paper,
tell the people with no goals I don't want to be you
so I'll see you later.

If you don't hear you can do it or I believe in you often
well you just heard it from me,
keep your head up and get your college degree.

THE SHOE DOES FIT

It's cool to be you right,
I'm trying to get the keys so I can be in tune like.

I was told all the love things,
I smiled because I believed it,
but it was a lie of things.

I know all things end, I didn't think this soon,
but eventually,
if you told me I would get stabbed in the back it wouldn't be
know convincing me.

I put the blame on me,
so shame on me,
you let me fall and I let you lean on me.

You got what you wanted by any means so are you happy now,
you uplift and praise the next,
while at the same time you put me down.

That fantasy life you wanted is it happening,
your friends your family think it's ok to do what you did,
I get crucified and hated for reacting to something you did.
I got motivation out of a bad situation,

I learned patience,
from being a hospital patient.

It's not me who's the problem because your it,
and if my words have you offended by it,
then I'm talking about you so wear it cause the shoe does fit.

Inner Me

Many chances I had that I blew,
colors in my face are unfamiliar like I never knew,
they say speak only when you're being spoken too,
I'm paranoid so I need a smoke or two,
I cry but the tears you'll never see,
that's why my face frowned up from the pain that's in me,
plenty woman want good but only attract bad,
I guess that's me so they feelings go first then they body follow
and leave me in the past,
only thing that's left is a broken heart of shattered glass
and picking up the pieces is hurt that'll always last,
I can't kiss you hold or do what you want me too,
like I said in the beginning these are moments that I blew,
I can be hood or a gentleman what ever you looking for, I can
give you less or give you more,
I never knew what it was to be a freak,
until I got older and I made it apart of me so the ladies
wouldn't pass me,
I'm the guy in the crowd that you never notice,
I'm the guy who only you I'm focused,
I pray you forgive me,
I can change just gotta kill the inner me.

POEM DESCRIPTIONS

INVISIBLE
This poem is about a person who is very aware of things, wants to speak out, but nobody has an ear to listen so he or she feels invisible.

JUST AIN'T RIGHT
This poem is about a girl with low self-esteem because of her father.

GUILTY
This poem is about admitting my faults, my wrong doing before anyone ask.

LAID IT ALL OUT
This poem is about me describing my personality and how I am towards myself and others.

A LIL CONFUSED
This poem is about a man not understanding why females select the type of guys that they do.

DON'T CRY
This poem is a dedication poem to those who lost someone unexpectedly do to a tragedy.

HONEST
This poem is about being honest with yourself.

ALONE
This poem is about figuring out things in life and not wanting to be alone to handle things.

MY CONFESSION
This poem is about sharing some mental secrets.

QUIET PLACE
This poem is about finding peace within yourself.

I DON'T GET IT
This poem is about not understanding the choices that most people make.

COLLEGE DEGREE
This poem is about encouraging people to go to school and get that degree to better the life they want.

The Shoe Does Fit
This poem is about removing the blame off the person who the hurt was done to, onto the person who caused it.

Inner Me
This poem is about expressing how I see myself on the inside, looking at my life on the outside.

IT'S PERSONAL

REALITY

THIS IS LIFE

Early mornings from sleepless nights,
calm thoughts after horrible fights,
citizens of a country with no rights,
addicted to alcohol weed and crack pipes.

Only escape from pain is too pretend laugh,
all this killing we got showers of tears and a blood bath.

Society subtract the blacks add stress divide races multiply the
time we get for a crime we didn't commit.

They want power, they want control,
so they present us with fear,
they said we was free from slavery,
but we not out the clear.

It's too many hurtful people,
it's too many heartless people,
it's too many selfish people,
it's too many gender swapping,
it's too many guns popping,
it's too many caskets dropping,
it's too many protest,

but the violence not stopping.
We all the same,
but none of us are treated equal,
it's gonna be another part of the same thing
so stay tuned for the sequel.

They making rules
and making laws
that's not right
it's like our hopes
and dreams
should get out our mind and far from sight,
our ancestors payed the way
and we still paying the price,
but the fact of the matter is,
this is life.

IT IS WHAT IT IS

Pills on the pull up, got drugs for your system let's do wrong
towards people and yell we the victim.

> Destroy and murder our own kind
> gotta be a must, point a finger at
> the whites as the
> blame when the blame is us.

They say education is the key to success,
 but is it the same if I get blessed.

> Girls want girls and guys want
> guys, they say lies is truth and the
> truth is lies.

The people with power, all they want is more power
and the less fortunate gone stay broke
that's just how that goes.

> The struggle is real this the life we
> was given, not the one we chose,
> we get surprised with yes cause
> we use to no's.

It's Crazy how strangers become friends
and friends become use to knows.

We make negative music
and say that's life, why not
make positive music to
save a life.
It's a harsh world and full of cold hearted people,
we are all divided so are we still equal.

They say forgive and
forget, but we forget to
forgive, I know our actions
bring the ones who really
care to tears, it's sad to say
it'll be no changes in this
world so it is what it is.

BLOWING OFF STEAM

First off pause and now press play,
get on your knees make a wish,
after that just pray,
cause the city is a war zone and nobody wants to stay.

We part of the food chain,
nobody is the predator,
we only the prey.

You got people making people
so who the real and who the fake.

We fall for words not actions call that bait.

We settle for happy meals,
and not the A1 sauce with steak.

Crazy how people turn their
back on us after one mistake,
they claim it was too much
and only so much more they can take,
women cheat on us
and say we the reason why
cause the truth
they can't face.

They clear they conscious with excuses and leave us with the
heartache
and wonder why men become dogs,
that's just the result after a heart break.

Call me iron fist cause they both glow,
in a room full of potential so I have to go.

Heart and mind in two different places,
I feel as if I lost a part of me or I could have misplaced it,
I cant be still I keep shaking.

They tell me smile cause you look mean,
I'm a free agent and I want to be on a team,
not having an answer makes me want to scream,
never mind what I'm saying,
I'm just blowing off steam.

UP 2 YOU AND ME

Everyday waking up wanting to change,
but day after day it's still the same.

Clocking in for work don't work for me
so I rather sale dope,
it's a recycle life style
so tell me where's hope,
I try to get out but it drags me back in by the neck with a rope,
I reach for it to get it lose cause I'm beginning to choke.

Mama told me
son grow up
and
do something with your life,
I had no father
so I was confused
by what I saw is it wrong or right,
I had no license no money for a car so I stole a bike.

Hanging out on the streets daily
no such thing as day and night,
everyday same thing party drink and we love to fight,
if you not from our hood you getting robbed on sight,
after we get what we want take a hike.

Get five guys tented windows in a car hitting blocks we slow
down cause we spot the opps, roll the window down drive off

fast after multiple pops, at this very moment I wanted out but it's too late cause we surrounded by cops.
Walking out to court room suit on in cuffs,
I didn't rat my friends out
so this process going to be rough,
no time for sensitive actions I have to be tough,
six months later
I learned my lesson,
jail I had enough.

I told the judge this really hurts my mom's to see me like this,
I can't go to prison,
I have to be here for her.

The judge said,
"You shouldn't have thought about your friends, should've thought about her."

I left the court room with a guilty plea,
I took the 25yrs and I took it happily,
understand life choices not up to friends or your family,
because everything we do is up 2 you and me.

HARD TO SEE

Sunday morning come along all
of a sudden I'm thinking how I did wrong
and life is lived short never to be long,
I walk in the building he preach about healing,
I get in my feelings,
I question my life and the things I deal with,
I'm skeptical but I have to be logical,
     every Sunday I have to be here
       that's my schedule.

Come across the pulpit saying God is watching you
    but when I look up I see nobody
      so how do I know it's true?

I'm lost I need a clue it's communion day
so we get a cracker and juice,
     now that I'm done
       what should I say or do?

He tell us confess our sins,
doing it in front of the congregation got me on
       needles and pins.

Tell him I can't do it and he say yea you can,
you family to us son not just a friend,
    this the beginning
     you'll appreciate it in the end.

I told the building sins   I did one, two, over three,
I live a sloppy life nothing I do is neat,
I'm tortured by my own dreams I'm afraid to sleep,
          life isn't real it just couldn't be.

Preacher rubs my back saying,
      "God always there,
           he forgives me,
              he cares and he loves me."

I told him that couldn't be facts but it's a possibility,
so what I'm gonna do is take my blinders off
        cause right now,
          what he saying to me it's hard to see.

QUESTIONS

What kind of world are we living in?

Is everybody God,
is that why people judge our sins?

Why most of your enemies have to be your undercover friend?

Why can't life go on and just has to end?

Why people can't be real,
                    they have to pretend?

Why people prefer a wave
                a handshake and not a hug,
                        or expressing so much hate
                                instead of showing love?

Why jobs have to pay less
then what we need and give us no right to succeed,
but we get the right bleed?

Why so many people homeless and helpless
then soon as you try to help them,
they say they can't help it,
if you ask me they're being selfish.

Why people can't express their mind,
is it because when you stand up they quick to offer you time,
the kind that will blow your mind?

Leave you in a dark room never again to see the sun shine.

Can't trust a women even though she seem fine,
            just know loyalty is rare and hard to find.

Why does it have to hurt even though it's a valuable lesson?

I'm not ungrateful so I thank God for his blessing,
            I know I shouldn't ask but I got a lot of questions.

VERDICT

Don't know how many times I have to say it,
how many times I have to claim it,
how close I have to aim it,
how many times I wish to change it,
how long I been waiting to say I made it,
how long I been waiting for a celebration
of something I created,
how many times I thought of forgetting things that I hated.

How long my misery gon' be others entertainment,
how many more people have to die that I hang with?

How many more black robe people think they can judge me,
how many brothers behind bars
cause of black skin and they not guilty,
how many people say I understand but they don't feel me?

How much longer are we going to criticize what's going on
before things start to change,
how long are we going to preach unity,
before we stop sending people back from where they came?

They figure we dealt with it before so we can keep on hurting,
let us kill ourselves off
because to them we will no longer be a burden,

how long we gone live thinking people really got our backs
when it's not for certain, I know it feel real but that real isn't
real so keep on searching.

The show just getting started with us speaking up
but they always find a way to close the curtain,
no matter what we do positive as a people
negativity gon' always be the verdict.

MINDSET

Decisions
      being made
           with your heart at stake,
they do wrong by you
      and down the line regret
          the choice they make,
         crazy you gotta change you
              from what they consider lame
                    to a thug,
           just for a woman to give you love.

Street life fast lane is what these females attracted too,
she say it's me and I'm sorry cause I don't deserve you,
yet you constantly hear where the real men at
and when they have it they run from truth,
that no good guy is who she really wants and not you.

See females nowadays don't want your time or your loyalty
cause it's nothing to fight for, they want that other guy who
get plenty women simply cause he got more.

You can be the best guy and do all you can,
but she still gone choose the other guy
cause she think he's the better man.

Give her what she want,

what ever she ask for and she still want stay,
           she'll find any excuse just to walk away.

Everything you do is underappreciated
           and your effort won't be enough
           compared to the guy that's next,
           none of this make sense,
           but this is the average female mindset.

MR. PRESIDENT

I see no changes, everyone one before said we are going to
change that and change this,
but as you see,
change doesn't seem to exist.

We steady losing lives, over lies,
caught up in the mix and can't be untied.

Need more jobs better pay,
we all speak but they don't listen to what we say.

Give monthly funds to those who really need it cause of they
health and they need help,
think about them and not just yourself.

The homeless need a home not a place where they can only lay,
they leave at a certain time they can't stay.

You a judge
be a judge
and if you a lawyer be a lawyer
stay in your place,
don't give out or offer a lighter sentence cause of skin color
and race.

Let's increase limitations so people can survive

cause the way it is now you can't make a living and still provide.

I been in your shoes and I'm still living it cause I'm a resident, vote for me and I'll be your Mr. President.

TALK ABOUT YOU

Look at this guy, he talks like this walks like this.

Not trying to take shots I'm trying to purposely miss,
people never think,
they hear what they hear,
and immediately think it's a diss.

Watch people say here he go again,
he need help he need a friend,
the things I been through
and everything I know you wouldn't comprehend.

I had a chip on my shoulder,
I brushed it off but I left crumbs behind,
now I have to talk about things just to ease my mind.

People only talk about others to get laughs for they own low
self esteem,
you can clearly see it,
there's no in between.

Keep your head up never down,
all the jokes they make don't be afraid to embrace it,
it takes a lot of guts to stay humble and face it,
take on the challenge get practice with the basic.
People are human like you,

so never get spooked, just as the grass is green and the sky is
blue,
you can count on people
to talk about you.

BULLY

So you think
cause I act different
and walk different
that makes me less of a person then you,
you think if
I lie I won't get in trouble like you,
I go to work and school for the same purpose as you.

I work to make money
and go to school to learn
and if we both touch fire wont we both get burned?

You laugh cause I'm skinny
and cause I prefer one friend over not having any.

You laugh cause you got and I don't,
you laugh cause I rather be myself and you wont.

One day we'll both be in a casket
soon to be six feet under
driven by hearses.

You're the same as me,
so what makes you perfect?

I want pull a gun out the bag,

shoot up the school,while wearing a hoodie,
I'm going to stand up to the man,
who trying to be a bully.

SMILE AGAIN

I lost my job,
lost my car,
and I lost my whole family,
no money coming,
no place to live,
man these things damaged me.

Have you ever lived in a world
full of people but still feel lonely?

I know it's me I see,
it's me,
but it's...
just something else inside me.

When I look in the mirror I don't see a reflection of me,
what ever or who ever it is hides me and maybe that's why
nobody notice me.

I been depressed,
I been stressed,
and I had times of feeling like a mess.

I had pills I should've took,
thought about it everyday and all night,
I wanted to slice the wrist,
but for some reason I couldn't find a knife.

I grabbed a gun
put it to my head
but I couldn't pull the trigger to end this life.

I heard a voice in my head
it was so loud as if the person had a mic,
it told me stop thinking
how I think and get my mind right.

I took it out on my family,
cause my boss told me
thank you for your work
but I'm sorry you're dismissed,
I couldn't believe after ten years I got dissed,
I came home said words I didn't mean cause I was pissed.

I tried to apologize by giving my wife a hug and a kiss,
she was so mad that she threw her ring
and said it's bout time we split.

I felt I wasn't a man,
cause I couldn't provide,
I felt poor,
thought I lost it all with the job,
but I really lost it all when my family walked out the door.

The day I thought would never happen did,
I got me another job got my family back,
and now I get to smile again.

POEM DESCRIPTIONS

THIS IS LIFE
This poem is about being in America and showing just how things are.

IT IS WHAT IT IS
This poem is about society, community, and us as a people on how we survive.

BLOWING OFF STEAM
This poem is about being fed up with society, with bad relationships and being treated like an outcast.

UP 2 YOU AND ME
This poem is about a young man who made a bad decision because he wanted to be like everybody else.

HARD TO SEE
This poem is about a guy who doesn't really believe in God or feel God loves him because of how he lives his life.

QUESTIONS
This poem is about having many questions of everything that goes on in life.

VERDICT
This poem is about how we are already charged or targeted with no chance of proving other wise.

MIND SET
This poem is about females not really being in the right state of mind when making decisions.

MR. PRESIDENT
This poem is speaking on if I was to be a president, these are some of the things I would change.

TALK ABOUT YOU
This poem is about understanding people are going to talk about you in a positive way or negative way no matter what.

BULLY
This poem is about standing up for yourself against a bully and showing you're both equal.

SMILE AGAIN
This poem is about a man who lost his job and told the story of how him taking his anger out on the wrong people affected him.